Paleo Diet for Cyclists

Delicious Paleo Diet Plan, Recipes and Cookbook for Achieving Optimum Health, Performance, Endurance and Physique Goals (Food for Fitness Series)

Lars Andersen

Published by Nordic Standard Publishing

Atlanta, Georgia USA

NORDICSTANDARD
PUBLISHING

ISBN 978-1-484145-24-1

Lars Andersen

Copyright © 2012 Lars Andersen

What Our Readers Are Saying

"Great to finally see someone tailoring the paleo diet to my specific needs"

★★★★☆ **Patrick F. Daniels (Marion Heights, PA)**

"Really good guide for people who want to eat healthy and improve their performance - Like me!"

★★★★★ **Helen G. Leigh (Bostwick, FL)**

"Easy to follow yet packed with information. Tasty too!"

★★★★★ **Bryan J. Meridith (Arch Cape, OR)**

Exclusive Bonus Download: Crossfit to Drop Fat

CrossFit is the principal strength and conditioning program for many police academies and tactical operations teams, military special operations units, champion martial artists, and hundreds of other elite and professional athletes worldwide.

Inside this ebook you will learn:

- The history of Cross fit training
- What is Cross fit training
- Advice on how to live life to the fullest yet still shred pounds
- Practical advice on the best exercises for cross fit
- The benefits of cross fit training
- Tips to help you succeed
- and more...

Go to the end of this book for the download link for this Bonus!

Thank you for downloading my book. Please REVIEW this book on Amazon. I need your feedback to make the next edition better. Thank you so much!

Books by Lars Andersen

The Smoothies for Runners Book

Juices for Runners

Smoothies for Cyclists

Juices for Cyclists

Paleo Diet for Cyclists

Smoothies for Triathletes

Juices for Triathletes

Paleo Diet for Triathletes

Smoothies for Strength

Juices for Strength

Paleo Diet for Strength

Paleo Diet Smoothies for Strength

Smoothies for Golfers

Juices for Golfers

Table of Contents

Disclaimer

While all attempts have been made to provide effective, verifiable information in this Book, neither the Author nor Publisher assumes any responsibility for errors, inaccuracies, or omissions. Any slights of people or organizations are unintentional.

This Book is not a source of medical information, and it should not be regarded as such. This publication is designed to provide accurate and authoritative information in regard to the subject matter covered. It is sold with the understanding that the publisher is not engaged in rendering a medical service. As with any medical advice, the reader is strongly encouraged to seek professional medical advice before taking action.

The Paleo Diet for Cyclists

Chemicals, n: Noxious substances from which modern foods are made. – Author Unknown

The Paleo diet is the common name given to the Paleolithic diet, so named because of its similarities to the diet of our hunter-gatherer ancestors some 2.5 million years ago in the Paleolithic Era. In essence, it's a diet that revolves around eating foods which occur naturally and avoiding foods which would be unrecognizable to a Paleolithic caveman! A popular rule of thumb proposed by Paleo advocates is, "If it's in a box, you shouldn't be eating it."

The current US Department of Agriculture (USDA) healthy eating guidelines promote a balanced daily diet consisting of 60 percent carbohydrates, 30 percent fats, and 10 percent protein. Switching from USDA recommendations to a Paleo diet will generally lead to an increase in your overall protein and fat intake and a drop in your overall carbohydrate intake. However, your main sources of carbohydrates will be fruits and vegetables, meaning that you will gain a plentiful supply of healthful micro-nutrients, and your main sources of protein will be lean meats with low levels of saturated fat, and fish with high levels of omega-3 essential fatty acids.

Cutting all "modern" foodstuffs from your diet, including all forms of grain as well as highly processed convenience foods, leaves a diet of all natural foodstuffs, for example:

- **Meat** – grass-fed rather than grain-fed animal sources.
- **Fowl** – chicken, turkey, duck, and game birds.
- **Fish** – wild fish rather than farmed fish as the latter can contain unhealthy levels of mercury and other toxins.
- **Eggs**
- **Vegetables** – excluding modern farmed varieties.
- **Oils** – any natural source such as olive oil, coconut oil, walnut oil, or avocado oil.
- **Fruits** – berries in particular and other fruits in moderation.
- **Nuts** – excluding peanuts.
- **Tubers** – sweet potatoes and yams in particular.

There is no *one* Paleo diet, and it's important to note that a Paleo-based diet is not necessarily a "low-carb diet" as such. Some hunter-gatherer populations would have survived and thrived on a low-carb diet; others would have lived equally well on a high-carb diet of fish, tubers, and coconut. An important element of all Paleo-based diets is that locally sourced organic produce should make up the bulk of your daily food intake whenever possible. However, this can prove expensive in some areas of today's world, so aiming to eat the best quality produce you can afford is an important step in terms of getting the most from a Paleo diet.

All You Can Eat!

The basic principle behind a Paleo diet is to eat only natural foodstuffs and to effectively eat all you want! There's no calorie counting or portion control required on a Paleo-based weight loss diet because a diet which is high in protein but low in sugar and starch (carbohydrate) prompts your body to burn fat for energy – a natural process known as ketosis. This can be an effective way to lose weight but in terms of eating a Paleo diet to fuel and maximize cycling performance, it's all about tailoring your carbohydrate intake to match your activity levels. If you are in serious training for a long-distance competitive event, your need for "starchy" carbohydrate fuel may increase in comparison to fuelling your body for leisure cycling activities. The most common sources of starchy carbs for Paleo cyclists are sweet potato and potato, although rice and quinoa may be included on occasion when energy demands are high.

Paleo Fuel Sources

Paleo "purists" eat only foods which can be hunted, fished or gathered. Foods include meat, offal, seafood, eggs, insects, fruits, nuts, seeds, vegetables, mushrooms, herbs and spices. Excluded foods include grains, legumes – beans and peanuts – dairy products, refined sugar, salt and processed oils. However, other Paleo-based diets include "modern" foods which were not available to our cavemen ancestors but support the macronutrient composition of a Paleolithic diet none-the-less. These foods include milk and dairy products, rice, potatoes and some processed oils such as olive oil or canola oil.

Protein

Meat sources:

Beef – with the exception of fiber, beef contains most of the nutrients your body needs:

- Calcium- essential for strong bones and teeth, and plays an important role in nerve transmission and muscle functions.
- Vitamin C – needed to make collagen, a protein essential for healthy gums, teeth, bones, cartilage and skin. Also aids the absorption of iron from plant food and is an important antioxidant. Antioxidants protect against free radicals, potentially harmful chemicals which are formed by your body as a by-product of its metabolic processes.
- Folate – needed for the formation of proteins in the body.
- Iron – an essential component of hemoglobin, the oxygen carrying pigment in red blood cells, and also important in energy metabolism.
- Iodine – vital for the production of thyroid hormones which govern the efficiency of converting food into energy.
- Manganese – a vital component of many enzymes involved in energy production.
- Zinc – vital for normal growth and development, and plays an important role in the functioning of the immune system.
- Selenium – an antioxidant which protects against free radical damage.
- Chromium – monitors blood sugar levels and stimulates glucose uptake in cells. Also helps to control fat and cholesterol levels in the blood.
- Silicon – required for strong, flexible joints and connective tissues.

The vitamin and mineral content of beef depends on the soil grazed. Grass-fed beef provides far greater health benefits than grain-fed beef. Lean beef contains less than five percent fat, half of which is saturated fat.

Lamb – provides a rich source of protein, B vitamins, zinc and iron.

Pork – one of the leanest meat sources of protein; lower in fat than beef and lamb. An excellent source of B vitamins:

- B vitamins – play an important role in releasing energy from food.
- Vitamin B12 – essential for all growth and division of cells, and for red cell formation.
- Also a useful source of zinc and iron.

Offal – ox liver and calves' liver are rich sources of easily absorbed iron. Also:

- Vitamin A – needed for normal cell division and growth, and plays an important role in maintaining the mucous membranes of the respiratory, digestive and urinary tracts.
- Vitamin B12

Kidneys also provide a rich source of B12 and both liver and kidney are low in fat.

Game and Game Birds – provide excellent sources of protein, with a much lower fat content than domesticated animals. This category includes sources such as venison, rabbit, wild boar and pheasant. They offer a rich source of B vitamins and iron, also:

- Potassium – essential for the transmission of all nerve impulses, and works in conjunction with sodium to maintain a healthy fluid and electrolyte balance within the cells. Electrolytes are charged particles that circulate in the blood, helping to regulate the body's fluid balance.
- Phosphorus – essential for the absorption of many nutrients, and plays a vital role in the release of energy in cells.

Wild game, when available, represents a chemical free source of protein compared to farmed game, but sources must always be sustainable.

Other animal sources:

Fish – all forms of fish provide excellent sources of protein, however, wild varieties offer healthier options than farmed versions. This also applies to **seafood**, with organic sources of crab, oysters, shrimp, scallops, lobster mussels and clams representing healthier choices.

- **Oysters** – excellent source of zinc and copper, needed for healthy bone and connective tissue growth. Copper also helps the body to absorb iron from food and is present in many enzymes which protect against free radical damage.
- **Mussels** – rich source of iron and iodine.
- **Scallops** – rich source of selenium.

- **Crab** – good source of potassium and zinc; also contains magnesium, which assists in nerve impulses and is important for muscle contraction.
- **Shrimps** – rich source of iodine; also useful source of selenium and calcium.
- **Clams** – excellent source of iron and useful source of zinc.

Eggs – omega-3 enriched eggs offer an excellent source of protein and healthy fat; a large egg contains around 6-8 grams of protein and 5-7 grams of fat, around 2 grams of which is saturated fat. However, it's recommended that no more than six eggs should be consumed per week due to the high cholesterol content. A rich source of:

- Vitamin B12
- Choline (in yolks) – aids the transport of cholesterol in the blood and plays an important role in fat metabolism.

Plant sources:

Hemp – provides a good source of protein, a healthy balance of omega-3 and omega-6 essential fatty acids, and contains many B vitamins, vitamin A, calcium and iron. Also:

- Vitamin D – needed to absorb calcium and phosphorus.
- Vitamin E – an important antioxidant.
- Sodium – essential for nerve and muscle function, and works in conjunction with potassium to regulate the body's fluid balance.
- And dietary fiber.

Green leafy vegetables – greens provide a good source of plant protein along with many other health benefits:

- **Beet greens** – the leafy tops of beets contain calcium, iron and beta-carotene, a powerful antioxidant. Research has also found that consuming beets on a regular basis can enhance an athlete's tolerance to high-intensity exercise.
- **Collard greens** – a good source of omega-3 essential fatty acids which have anti-inflammatory properties.
- **Lettuce** – a good source of vitamin C, beta-carotene, folate, calcium and iron.
- **Mustard greens** – an excellent source of antioxidant vitamins A, C, E, and vitamin K which plays an essential role in the formation of certain proteins. Also contains carotenes and flavonoids which are powerful antioxidants, and calcium, iron, magnesium, potassium, zinc, selenium and manganese.
- **Swiss chard** – a rich source of vitamin A, C and K, B vitamins, omega-3 fatty acids, and a number of antioxidants and flavonoids. Also contains copper, calcium, sodium, potassium, iron, manganese and phosphorus.
- **Turnip greens** – a rich source of beta-carotene, vitamin C, and a useful source of folate.
- **Spinach** – a rich source of carotenoids, including antioxidants beta-carotene and lutein. Also contains vitamin C and potassium.

Cruciferous vegetables

- **Cabbage** - rich source of vitamin C, vitamin K, and a good source of vitamin E, potassium and beta-carotene. Vitamin K is essential in the formation of many proteins - the body's building blocks - and vitamin E has an important role to play in preventing free radical damage.
- **Broccoli** - another rich source of vitamin C. Broccoli also contains beta-carotene, iron and potassium, and is high in bioflavonoids and other antioxidants. Iron is essential for the production of hemoglobin, the oxygen carrying pigment in red blood cells, and myoglobin, a similar pigment which stores oxygen in your muscles.
- **Kale** - a good source of iron, calcium, vitamin C and beta-carotene.
- **Cauliflower** – a rich source of vitamin C.
- **Rutabaga** – a good source of vitamin A and iron.
- **Kohlrabi** – a good source of vitamin C, calcium, phosphorus and iron.
- **Watercress** – rich source of vitamin C, beta-carotene and iron.

Fats

Good quality fat sources in a Paleo-based diet are the saturated fats provided by grass-fed meat and the fat provided by organic eggs. The preferred cooking fats are tallow, lard, grass-fed butter, ghee, coconut oil, palm oil and perhaps olive oil, although processed oils should be avoided whenever possible and used for dressing foods rather than cooking foods. Some oils contain high levels of omega-6 fatty acids which can cause an inflammatory response in your body. For this reason, most nut and seed oils should be used sparingly. Macadamia nuts offer the lowest levels of omega-6 but alternatives include flax seed oil (linseed oil), walnut oil, avocado oil and canola.

Carbohydrates

Paleo carbohydrate sources are mainly fruits and vegetables. Carbohydrates can be split into two main categories: simple carbohydrates or **sugars**, and complex carbohydrates or **starches**. Starches provide a much slower release of energy compared to sugars, making them the preferred source of fuel for long-distance cycling activities. The natural sugar content of most fruits means they must be consumed in moderation to avoid sugar "spikes" and "crashes" whereas the majority of vegetables can be consumed on an "all you can eat" basis.

Good sources of Paleo carbohydrate include:

- **Cassava** – a good source of "starchy" carbohydrate. Also provides calcium, iron, manganese, phosphorus, potassium, B vitamins, vitamin C and dietary fiber. Cassava flour is gluten-free.
- **Taro root** – a starchy vegetable offering a rich source of potassium, and a useful source of calcium, vitamins C and E, B vitamins, manganese, magnesium and copper. Taro leaves are also relatively high in protein.
- **Plantains** – a good low sugar source of starchy carbohydrate, also an excellent source of potassium and dietary fiber, and a useful source of vitamins A and C.
- **Yam** – a good source of vitamin B6, vitamin C, potassium and manganese.

- **White potatoes** – a good source of starchy carbohydrate, protein and fiber. They also provide vitamin C and potassium.
- **Sweet potatoes** – a good source of vitamin B6, vitamin C, vitamin D, iron, magnesium, potassium and beta-carotene.
- **Squash** – a good source of vitamins C and A, and also a useful source of calcium and iron.

In moderation, the following fruits also provide a good source of carbohydrate:

- **Strawberries** - a rich source of vitamin C and also an aid to the absorption of iron from vegetables.
- **Pears** - a good source of vitamin C, potassium, pectin and bioflavonoids. Pectin provides fiber, and bioflavonoids are powerful antioxidants.
- **Mangoes** - a good source of vitamin C and beta-carotene.
- **Bananas** - a rich source of potassium.
- **Apple** – offers a small amount of vitamin C.
- **Peach** – a good source of vitamins A and C.
- **Blueberries** - often described as "the ultimate brain food," blueberries have an antioxidant content of around five times higher than other fruits and vegetables. Research has discovered that a daily serving of 100 grams can stimulate new brain cell growth and slow down the effects of mental ageing. Mental sharpness can provide a "winning edge" in competitive cycling events.

Both fruits and vegetables provide a healthful source of carbohydrates for energy but the added fiber content of vegetables helps to slow the absorption of sugar and thereby a slower and steadier release of energy is provided. Dark green leafy vegetables are nutritionally dense, making them an ideal source of energy to fuel endurance cycling sports.

Cycle Fuel

All carbohydrates are converted into glucose and glycogen before they can be used to fuel everyday activities and exercise. While cycling, the working muscles are fuelled by glucose in the blood, and by glycogen from stores in the liver and in the muscles. Glucose and glycogen are inter-convertible. When the body has a sufficient supply of glucose, carbohydrates are converted to glycogen and stored, but if glucose is in short supply, glycogen is converted to glucose ready for use.

During endurance sports such as long-distance cycling, the body conserves as much of its glycogen reserves as possible by using some of its fat stores for energy. However, compared to carbohydrate, fat is a very slow source of energy, meaning that as the intensity of the exercise increases, the body switches to using glycogen to provide a faster release of energy. Your body can only store a limited amount of glycogen, with the muscles able to store enough for up to around two hours of intense exercise. After exercising, your body's ability to store glycogen is elevated. This period of around 30 minutes is known as the "glycogen window" and consuming appropriate foods in this window helps replenish glycogen stores, promote muscle repair and restoration, and thereby aid recovery after a long or intense cycle ride.

The foods you eat fuel your body for cycling, they *do not* improve your cycling performance on their own! Eating lean meat does not instantly add lean muscle to your body. The only way to become a fitter cyclist is to cycle more, but quality is more important than quantity in cycle training terms. Shorter and more intense sessions, including hill work and intervals, are an important element of a performance training program, even for endurance cyclists. The quality foods you eat provide quality fuel for your body, allowing you to put in a quality effort in every training session. However, it's also crucial to remember the importance of rest and recovery. Active recovery rides at a leisurely pace of less than 75 percent of your maximum heart rate not only allow your body to regenerate after intense training, they maximize your body's use of fat as its main source of energy.

Carbohydrates are crucial to achieving a top endurance performance and replenishing glycogen stores after training is essential if energy levels are to be maintained. Eating a Paleo-based meal containing a mix of carbohydrates and protein is an ideal post-training source of energy-replenishing nutrients but it's not always possible to prepare or eat a full meal within the 30-minute glycogen window after a ride. A snack containing starchy carbohydrates such as potatoes or sweet potatoes prepared in advance can be a practical way to bridge the gap between finishing a ride and sitting down to eat a full meal. A green smoothie made with green, leafy vegetables and berries blended with water provides a convenient and nutritious alternative. If you choose to include some dairy products in your Paleo diet, adding milk or yogurt to a post-ride smoothie can boost the protein content. Milk contains whey protein which is fast-acting and helps to reduce the effects of muscle damage immediately after an intense ride, and casein protein which is slow-acting and helps to continue the repair process long after the ride.

Fuel with Flavor!

The list of non-Paleo foods to avoid often seems much longer than the list of foods which *can* be eaten when choosing to follow a Paleo-based diet. However, as just one example, a Paleo meal could be grass-fed lamb broiled with a hint of rosemary and served with chard sautéed in bacon ends. That's a flavorsome meal! If you need additional carbohydrates to fuel your cycling activities, adding potatoes smothered in grass-fed butter to your plate is a tasty way to meet those needs.

The use of fresh herbs can add a flavorsome twist to your meals or to a green smoothie with the additional benefit of boosting the nutritional content. Popular choices include:

- **Parsley** - one cup of parsley contains 2 grams of protein. It is also rich in calcium and provides iron, copper, magnesium, potassium, zinc, phosphorus, beta-carotene and vitamin C.
- **Dill** – adds a sweet flavor to foods and contains calcium, iron, manganese, vitamin C, and beta-carotene.
- **Sorrel** - provides iron, magnesium and calcium.
- **Basil** - provides beta-carotene, iron, potassium, copper, manganese and magnesium
- **Cilantro (Coriander)** - provides a mild, peppery flavor along with anti-inflammatory properties, vitamin C, iron and magnesium.

Other Paleo sources of nutrition and flavor include:

- **Bell peppers**
- **Eggplants**
- **Mushrooms**
- **Onions**
- **Radishes**
- **Tomatillos**
- **Cucumber**
- And if you have a sweet tooth, **raspberries** or **Brazil nuts** covered in **organic dark chocolate** make a delicious treat!

In most Paleo-based diets, nuts and seeds can be eaten in moderation. Popular choices include almonds, macadamia nuts, walnuts, cashews, chestnuts, pine nuts, pecans, unsalted pistachios, sunflower seeds, pumpkin seeds and sesame seeds. Many Paleo advocates believe that all caffeine sources should be avoided but others include coffee and tea in moderation when prepared without the addition of sugar.

5 Steps to Paleo Pedal Power

A Paleo-based diet is essentially a diet which revolves around consuming moderate amounts of meat, moderate amounts of fruit and unlimited amounts of vegetables.

Becoming a Paleo-fuelled cyclist can be summarized as follows:

- **Eat only real food** – buy locally grown, fresh, organic produce whenever possible.
- **Do not eat any processed or refined carbohydrates** – avoid sugar, flour, pasta, bread and candy. Eat fruits for sweet flavors or honey occasionally if your activity levels require an extra energy boost.
- **Eat plenty of high quality fat** – sources include meat, eggs, avocado and also dairy if you choose to include it. Avoid processed oils and industrial meats, and eat nuts in moderation to help keep a healthy omega-3 and omega-6 balance.
- **Eat only high quality meat** – buy grass-fed or wild sources whenever possible; organ meats provide cost-effective sources of quality protein.
- **Tailor your non-refined carbohydrate intake to match your activity levels** – eat as many starchy vegetables as you like, potatoes and sweet potatoes in moderation, rice or quinoa only when energy demands are high, and avoid all grains containing gluten.

Paleo recipes – Cyclists

Breakfasts

Chocolate pancake with fresh strawberry syrup

Preparation time	15 minutes
Ready time	40 minutes
Serves	4
Serving quantity/unit	189 G / 7 Ounces
Calories	357 Cal
Total Fat	26.2 g
Cholesterol	126 mg
Sodium	61 mg
Total Carbohydrates	23.8 g
Dietary fibers	7.4g
Sugars	12.8g
Protein	14.2g
Vitamin C	0.71
Vitamin A	0.04
Iron	0.17
Calcium	0.16

Ingredients

Pancakes

- 3 organic eggs
- ½ cup of grass-fed milk or almond milk
- 1 ½ cups of almond meal
- 4 tbsps. of raw cocoa
- 1 tbsp. of unsweetened apple sauce
- 1 tbsp. of coconut oil, melted

Strawberry syrup

- 2 cups of strawberries
- 3 tbsps. of water
- 4 tsps. of raw honey

Method

Pancakes:

- Pre-heat a non-stick pan.
- Combine the eggs, milk, almond flour, cocoa and applesauce in a large bowl and mix.
- Brush the pan with the coconut oil and pour in ¼ to 1/3 of batter, cook for 2 or 3 minutes, until bubbles burst on the surface, turn and cook the other side for 1 minute or until golden.

Strawberry syrup:

- Combine the strawberries and water in a medium saucepan and bring to a simmer.
- Simmer for 10-15 minutes or until the strawberries are soft and the syrup is thickened, add the raw honey and remove from heat.
- Serve the pancakes with the strawberry syrup spooned on top.

Carrot and raisins bread

Preparation time	15 minutes
Ready time	55 minutes
Serves	6
Serving quantity/unit	100 G / 4 ounces
Calories	329 Cal
Total Fat	23 g
Cholesterol	82 mg
Sodium	359 mg
Total Carbohydrates	28g
Dietary fibers	4g
Sugars	21g
Protein	8g
Vitamin C	0.02
Vitamin A	0.69
Iron	0.09
Calcium	0.09

Ingredients

- 1 ½ cups of almond meal
- 1 tsp. of baking soda
- 1 tsp. of cinnamon
- ¾ cup of boiled carrots
- 1/3 cup of raw honey
- ¼ cup of coconut oil, melted
- 3 organic eggs
- ¼ cup of raisins

Method

- Preheat oven to 350F.
- Mash the carrots.
- Combine the almond meal, baking soda and cinnamon in a food processor. Add the carrots, honey, oil and organic eggs to the flour mixture and pulse until the batter is homogenous. Add the raisins.
- Scoop the batter into a small loaf pan. Bake for 35-40 minutes or until a toothpick comes out clean.

Banana and almond butter muffin

Preparation time	15 minutes
Ready time	1 hour
Serves	8
Serving quantity/unit	118 G / 4 ounces /1 muffin
Calories	383 Cal
Total Fat	30 g
Cholesterol	83mg
Sodium	355mg
Total Carbohydrates	21g
Dietary fibers	6g
Sugars	10g
Protein	13g
Vitamin C	0.04
Vitamin A	0.03
Iron	0.12
Calcium	0.14

Ingredients

- 4 organic eggs, yolks and whites separated
- 3 tbsps. of coconut oil, melted
- 2 tbsps. of raw honey
- 3 tbsps. of almond butter
- 6 tbsps. of grass-fed milk or almond milk
- 2 medium bananas, mashed
- 3 ¼ cups of almond flour
- 1 tsp. of baking soda

Method

- Preheat the oven to 350°F.
- Combine the yolks, oil, honey and almond butter in a large bowl and add the milk.
- Mix flour with baking soda and add to the organic egg mixture.
- Beat the organic egg whites until stiff and carefully fold them in the cake batter.
- Pour the batter into paper muffin liners and bake for 45 minutes or until a toothpick comes out clean.

Blueberry squares

Preparation time	15 minutes
Ready time	1 hour
Serves	8
Serving quantity/unit	118 G / 4 ounces /1 muffin
Calories	383 Cal
Total Fat	30 g
Cholesterol	83mg
Sodium	355mg
Total Carbohydrates	21g
Dietary fibers	6g
Sugars	10g
Protein	13g
Vitamin C	0.04
Vitamin A	0.03
Iron	0.12
Calcium	0.14

Ingredients

- ¾ cup of almonds
- ¾ cup of cashew
- ¾ cup of dried coconut flakes
- 2 tbsps. of flax seed
- 2 tbsps. of raw honey
- 4 tbsps. of almond butter
- 1 tbsp. of grass-fed milk or almond milk
- 1 organic egg
- 1 cup of blueberries

Method

- Preheat oven to 350°F.
- Pulse the flax seeds in a food processor until grind, transfer into a small bowl and add two tablespoons of water. Set aside.
- Pulse the almonds, cashews and half of the coconut flakes in a food processor until very finely chopped.
- Combine the honey, almond butter, organic egg, flax seed mixture and milk in a large bowl. Add the almond mixture and blend. Finally, incorporate the remaining coconut and the blueberries in the batter.
- Press the batter into a small square/rectangular baking pan previously lined with non-stick baking paper.
- Bake for 15-20 minutes. Let cool and cut into squares.

Pumpkin Smoothie

Preparation time	5 minutes
Ready time	5 minutes
Serves	4
Serving quantity/unit	330 G / 11 ounces
Calories	272 Cal
Total Fat	12g
Cholesterol	0mg
Sodium	79mg
Total Carbohydrates	40g
Dietary fibers	9g
Sugars	18g
Protein	8g
Vitamin C	0.11
Vitamin A	3.07
Iron	0.26
Calcium	0.09

Ingredients

- 2 cups of unsweetened organic pumpkin puree
- 2 cups of almond milk
- 2 cups of banana
- 2 tsps. of pumpkin pie spice
- ½ cup of almonds
- 4 tbsps. of pumpkin seeds
- 4 tbsps. of raw cocoa

Method

- Combine all the ingredients in a food processor and pulse until smooth.

Cinnamon roll

Preparation time	20 minutes
Ready time	45 minutes
Serves	8
Serving quantity/unit	110 G / 4 ounce / 1 roll
Calories	370 Cal
Total Fat	28g
Cholesterol	62mg
Sodium	345 mg
Total Carbohydrates	25g
Dietary fibers	7g
Sugars	16g
Protein	12g
Vitamin C	0.02
Vitamin A	0.02
Iron	0.12
Calcium	0.14

Ingredients

Roll:

- 3 ½ cups of almond meal/flour
- 1 tbsp. of raw honey
- 1/3 tbsp. of coconut oil, melted
- 1 pinch of nutmeg
- 2 tsps. of cinnamon
- 3 organic eggs
- 3 tbsps. of grass-fed milk or almond milk
- 1 tsp. of baking soda

Filling:

- 8 tbsps. of pecan nuts, chopped
- 1 apple, finely chopped
- 4 tbsps. of raw honey
- 2 tsps. of cinnamon

Method

- Preheat oven to 350°F.
- Grease a rectangular pan with the oil and line with non-stick baking paper.
- Combine the eggs, oil, milk and honey in a large bowl.
- Pulse the almond meal in a food processor with the cinnamon, nutmeg and baking soda. Add to the egg mixture and blend.
- Press the batter into the pan.
- Place the filling ingredients evenly on the dough and roll up the dough using the baking paper.
- Cut the roll into eight portions using a sharp knife and bake for 20-25 minutes, or until golden brown.

Grilled bananas with pecan nuts and blackberry syrup

Preparation time	10 minutes
Ready time	25 minutes
Serves	4
Serving quantity/unit	230 G / 8 ounces
Calories	277 Cal
Total Fat	11 g
Cholesterol	0 mg
Sodium	3 mg
Total Carbohydrates	49 g
Dietary fibers	8 g
Sugars	31 g
Protein	4 g
Vitamin C	0.43
Vitamin A	0.05
Iron	0.07
Calcium	0.04

Ingredients

- 4 bananas, unpeeled
- Blackberry syrup:
- 2 cup of blackberries
- 3 tbsp. of raw honey
- 2 tbsp. of water

Serve with:

- 1/2 cup of pecan nuts, coarsely chopped

Method

Blackberry Syrup:

- Combine the blackberries and water in a medium saucepan and bring to a simmer.
- Let simmer for 10-15 minutes or until the blackberries are soft and the syrup thickens, add the honey and remove from heat.

Grilled bananas:

- Preheat an electric griller or a non-stick pan.
- Cut the unpeeled bananas lengthwise and grill for two or three minutes with the cut side down. Peel the bananas.
- Serve the banana halves topped with blackberry syrup and two tablespoons of pecan nuts for person.

Snacks

Tapenade

Preparation time	5 minutes
Ready time	5 minutes
Serves	4
Serving quantity/unit	148 G / 5 ounces
Calories	122 Cal
Total Fat	11 g
Cholesterol	0 mg
Sodium	500 mg
Total Carbohydrates	8 g
Dietary fibers	2g
Sugars	2g
Protein	1g
Vitamin C	0.1
Vitamin A	0.56
Iron	0.08
Calcium	0.05

Ingredients

Tapenade:

- 1 cup of pitted black olives
- 3 tbsps. of capers
- 2 tbsps. of olive oil
- 2 garlic cloves
- 1 tbsp. of lemon juice
- ½ tsp. of pepper

Serve with:

- 1 carrot, cut into strips
- 1 celery stalk, cut into strips
- 1 cucumber, cut into strips

Method

Tapenade:

- Combine all the ingredients for the tapenade in a food processor and pulse until smooth.
- Serve with the carrot, celery and cucumber strips.

Chocolate covered strawberries

Preparation time	15 minutes
Ready time	50 minutes
Serves	4
Serving quantity/unit	90 G / 3 ounces
Calories	106 Cal
Total Fat	7g
Cholesterol	0mg
Sodium	1mg
Total Carbohydrates	13g
Dietary fibers	3g
Sugars	8g
Protein	2g
Vitamin C	0.71
Vitamin A	0
Iron	0.04
Calcium	0.03

Ingredients

- 2 cups of strawberries, whole
- 2oz. (60g) organic dark chocolate

Method

- Melt the chocolate in a double boiler stirring frequently, until smooth.
- Meanwhile insert a toothpick into each strawberry and deep them into the melted chocolate.
- Place the strawberries on a sheet of parchment paper to cool, or turn the toothpick upside down, insert it into Styrofoam and let the chocolate cool.

Guacamole

Preparation time	5 minutes
Ready time	20 minutes
Serves	4
Serving quantity/unit	190 G / 7 ounces
Calories	142 Cal
Total Fat	11 g
Cholesterol	0mg
Sodium	312mg
Total Carbohydrates	12g
Dietary fibers	5g
Sugars	4g
Protein	2g
Vitamin C	0.29
Vitamin A	0.57
Iron	0.04
Calcium	0.03

Ingredients

Guacamole:

- 1 avocado
- 3 garlic cloves, finely chopped
- 1 tbsp. of coconut oil, melted
- ½ onion, finely chopped
- 3 tbsps. of lemon juice
- ½ tbsp. of fresh coriander, finely chopped
- 1 tomato, chopped
- ½ tsp. of salt
- ¼ tsp. of pepper

Serve with:

- 1 carrot, cut into strips
- 1 cucumber, cut into strips
- 1 celery stalk, cut into strips

Method

- Guacamole:
- Halve and pit the avocado and scoop out its meat from the peal.
- Transfer to a bowl and mash with a fork.
- Add the garlic, onion, cilantro, lemon, oil and coriander; mash some more.
- Add the chopped tomatoes immediately before serving.
- Serve the guacamole with the carrot, cucumber and celery strips.

Mango and passion fruit smoothie with romaine lettuce

Preparation time	5 minutes
Ready time	5 minutes
Serves	4
Serving quantity/unit	169 G / 6 ounces
Calories	115 Cal
Total Fat	1 g
Cholesterol	0 mg
Sodium	21 mg
Total Carbohydrates	29 g
Dietary fibers	8 g
Sugars	19 g
Protein	2g
Vitamin C	0.69
Vitamin A	0.3
Iron	0.06
Calcium	0.02

Ingredients

- 1 cup of passion fruit pulp
- 2 cups of mango
- 2 cups of romaine lettuce

Method

- Combine all the ingredients in a food processor and pulse until smooth.

Trail mix

Preparation time	5 minutes
Ready time	25 minutes
Serves	8
Serving quantity/unit	50 G / 2 ounces
Calories	181 Cal
Total Fat	8 g
Cholesterol	0 mg
Sodium	8 mg
Total Carbohydrates	27 g
Dietary fibers	5g
Sugars	19 g
Protein	3g
Vitamin C	0.01
Vitamin A	0.14
Iron	0.05
Calcium	0.05

Ingredients

- ½ cup of almonds
- ½ cup of pecan nuts
- ½ cup of dried apricots, chopped
- 8 slices of dried mango, chopped
- ½ cup of dried cherries, chopped

Method

- Preheat oven to 350F.
- Transfer the almonds and pecans into an oven safe dish lined with non-stick baking paper and roast for 15-20 minutes stirring occasionally. Let cool.
- Put the nuts and dried fruits in a large bowl and toss to combine.

Spinach and mushroom omelet muffin

Preparation time	15 minutes
Ready time	40 minutes
Serves	4
Serving quantity/unit	90 G / 3 ounces
Calories	92 Cal
Total Fat	6 g
Cholesterol	206 mg
Sodium	379 mg
Total Carbohydrates	2 g
Dietary fibers	1g
Sugars	1g
Protein	8g
Vitamin C	0.05
Vitamin A	0.2
Iron	0.08
Calcium	0.06

Ingredients

- 5 organic eggs, beaten
- 3 tbsps. of grass-fed milk or almond milk
- 1 cup of spinach
- ½ cup of mushrooms, chopped
- 2 tbsps. of onion, finely chopped
- 1 garlic clove, finely chopped
- 1 tsp. of rosemary
- ½ tsp. of salt
- ½ tsp. of pepper

Method

- Preheat the oven to 350F.
- Stir the eggs, milk, salt, pepper and rosemary in a large bowl until well blended.
- Prepare the filling combining the spinach, mushrooms, onion and garlic in a bowl. Place a small amount of filling into the bottom of muffin paper liners, pour egg mixture into each cup of and bake for 20-25 minutes or until muffins are light golden brown.

Zucchini chips

Preparation time	10 minutes
Ready time	2h10m
Serves	4
Serving quantity/unit	75 G / 3 ounces
Calories	86 Cal
Total Fat	7 g
Cholesterol	0 mg
Sodium	304 mg
Total Carbohydrates	6 g
Dietary fibers	1g
Sugars	2 g
Protein	2g
Vitamin C	0.37
Vitamin A	0.05
Iron	0.03
Calcium	0.03

Ingredients

- 2 ½ zucchinis, thinly sliced
- 2 tbsps. of olive oil
- 6 garlic cloves, finely chopped
- ½ tsp. of salt

Method

- Preheat oven to 175F and line baking sheets with non-stick baking paper.
- In a large bowl combine the zucchini, olive oil, garlic and salt.
- Lay the zucchini slices in the baking sheets and bake for around 2 hours or until crisp.

Celery stalks with almond butter and raw honey

Preparation time	5 minutes
Ready time	5 minutes
Serves	4
Serving quantity/unit	59 G / 2 ounces
Calories	148 Cal
Total Fat	12 g
Cholesterol	0 mg
Sodium	30 mg
Total Carbohydrates	10 g
Dietary fibers	1g
Sugars	5 g
Protein	3g
Vitamin C	0.02
Vitamin A	0.03
Iron	0.05
Calcium	0.07

Ingredients

- 8 celery stalks
- 1 tbsp. of raw honey
- 5 tbsps. of almond butter

Method

- Stir the honey and almond butter in a small bowl until well blended.
- Cut the celery stalks into 4 inch size pieces and spread one and a half teaspoon of the almond butter mixture into the celery pieces.

Lunches

Paleo Burger with sweet and sour vegetables

Preparation time	5 minutes
Ready time	5 minutes
Serves	4
Serving quantity/unit	590 G / 21 ounces
Calories	562 Cal
Total Fat	23 g
Cholesterol	119 mg
Sodium	234 mg
Total Carbohydrates	63 g
Dietary fibers	11 g
Sugars	41 g
Protein	33g
Vitamin C	3.08
Vitamin A	4.19
Iron	0.28
Calcium	0.15

Ingredients

Burger:

- 350g grass-fed beef, ground, 95% lean meat
- 1 organic egg
- 2 garlic cloves
- 2 tbsp. of olive oil
- Sweet and sour vegetables:
- 4 cups of broccoli, chopped

- 4 cups of pineapple, chopped
- 4 cups of carrot, sliced
- 1 onion, finely chopped
- 2 garlic cloves, finely chopped
- 4 tbsps. of raw honey
- 1 tbsp. of raw apple cider vinegar
- 2 tbsps. of olive oil

Method

Burger:

- Preheat the grill.
- Place the beef in a mixing bowl, add the remaining burger ingredients and stir to combine.
- Shape the burgers, using your hands, into 4 patties and grill for 10-15 minutes.
- Sweet and Sour vegetables
- Pour the olive oil into a large non-stick pan and sauté the onion and garlic until it is soft and translucent.
- Add the broccoli and carrots and cook for 5 minutes.
- Add the pineapple and cook for further 10 minutes.
- Stir the honey and vinegar in a small bowl until well blended. Add the mixture to the pan, stir, and cook for another 3-4 minutes.

Grilled peach, raisins and nuts salad

Preparation time	15 minutes
Ready time	30 minutes
Serves	4
Serving quantity/unit	450 G / 16 ounces
Calories	560 Cal
Total Fat	36 g
Cholesterol	0 mg
Sodium	275 mg
Total Carbohydrates	56 g
Dietary fibers	10 g
Sugars	32 g
Protein	16g
Vitamin C	1.14
Vitamin A	1.69
Iron	0.31
Calcium	0.25

Ingredients

- 8 cups of spinach
- 8 cups of watercress
- 1 cup of cashews
- 1 cup of almonds
- 8 peaches
- 8 tbsps. of raisins
- 1 red onion, chopped
- 2 tbsps. of olive oil
- ¼ cup of lemon juice
- ½ tsp. of pepper
- ½ tsp. of salt
- ¼ tsp. of chili powder

Method

- Preheat an electric griller or a non-stick pan.
- Stir the olive oil, lemon juice, pepper, salt and chili powder in a small bowl until well blended.
- Halve and pit the peaches Grill, covered, with the cut side down, for three or four minutes, or until tender. Let cool a little bit and then chop.
- Place the greens in a large bowl; add the onion, nuts, peaches and raisins. Toss to combine.
- Add the lemon dressing just before serving.

Beef skewers

Preparation time	20 minutes
Ready time	40 minutes
Serves	5
Serving quantity/unit	423 G / 15 ounces
Calories	362 Cal
Total Fat	19 g
Cholesterol	84 mg
Sodium	425 mg
Total Carbohydrates	20 g
Dietary fibers	4g
Sugars	10 g
Protein	30g
Vitamin C	1.18
Vitamin A	2.38
Iron	0.22
Calcium	0.07

Ingredients

Beef kebab:

- 1 pound of grass-fed beef sirloin, cubed
- 1 red bell pepper,
- 1 green bell pepper,
- 1 onion,
- 3 tbsps. of olive oil
- ½ tsp. of salt
- Serve with:

- 5 carrots, cut into strips
- 3 cucumbers, cut into strips
- 4 tbsp. of mayonnaise

Method

- Preheat the grill.
- Core the bell peppers and cut them into pieces for skewering. Cut the onions the same way.
- Season the olive oil with salt, pepper and other seasonings of your choice.
- Alternate pieces of meat and vegetables on metal skewers and grill for 5 minutes on each side, or until the meat is cooked to desired doneness, brushing each side with the olive oil dressing.

Smoked salmon wraps

Preparation time	15 minutes
Ready time	25 minutes
Serves	4
Serving quantity/unit	260 G / 9 ounces
Calories	167 Cal
Total Fat	6 g
Cholesterol	20 mg
Sodium	1819 mg
Total Carbohydrates	10.4 g
Dietary fibers	3 g
Sugars	5 g
Protein	18 g
Vitamin C	0.21
Vitamin A	1.99
Iron	0.09
Calcium	0.05

Ingredients

- 8 large lettuce leaves
- 1 ½ cups of tomato, chopped
- 2 cups of carrot, grated
- 2 tbsps. of Scallion, chopped
- ¾ cup of cucumber, cubed
- 12 oz. of smoked salmon (wild)
- 1/4 cup of olives, pitted

- 4 tbsp. of sunflower seeds
- ½ tsp. of pepper

Method

- Distribute the tomato, carrot, cucumber, scallion, olives and sunflower seeds evenly among the lettuce leaves.
- Top with the salmon and sprinkle with pepper.
- Wrap the lettuce and serve.

Warm cauliflower rice salad

Preparation time	15 minutes
Ready time	30 minutes
Serves	4
Serving quantity/unit	650 G / 23 ounces
Calories	316 Cal
Total Fat	14 g
Cholesterol	38 mg
Sodium	1100 mg
Total Carbohydrates	35 g
Dietary fibers	17g
Sugars	15 g
Protein	20g
Vitamin C	2.45
Vitamin A	0.21
Iron	0.15
Calcium	0.1

Ingredients

- 1 large cauliflower head, coarsely chopped
- 2 cups of ham, cubed
- 2 cups of mushrooms, chopped
- 2 organic eggplants, chopped
- 1 green bell pepper, chopped
- 1 onion, finely chopped
- 2 tbsps. of olive oil
- ¼ tsp. of salt
- ½ tsp. of pepper

Method

- Place the cauliflower in a food processor and pulse until it is the size of rice. Transfer to a microwave-safe dish, season with salt and pepper, cover, and microwave on high in periods of 5 minutes until tender (stirring and verifying the cauliflower consistency between each period).
- Transfer to a large mixing bowl and set aside.
- Pour the olive oil onto a non-stick pan, add the onion and cook until it's soft and translucent. Add the remaining vegetables and cook for further 8-10 minutes.
- Add the ham and cook for more 3 minutes.
- Add the vegetables and ham mixture to the cauliflower and toss to combine.

Shrimp omelet

Preparation time	15 minutes
Ready time	30 minutes
Serves	4
Serving quantity/unit	650 G / 23 ounces
Calories	316 Cal
Total Fat	14 g
Cholesterol	38 mg
Sodium	1100 mg
Total Carbohydrates	35 g
Dietary fibers	17g
Sugars	15 g
Protein	20g
Vitamin C	2.45
Vitamin A	0.21
Iron	0.15
Calcium	0.1

Ingredients

- 3 organic eggs
- 4 organic egg whites
- 6 tbsps. of grass-fed milk or almond milk
- 8 ounces of wild shrimp, peeled
- 3 tbsps. of scallions, chopped
- 1 tbsp. of parsley, finely chopped
- 1 red bell pepper, chopped
- 2 tbsps. of olive oil
- 1 tbsp. of lemon juice
- 1 tbsp. of fresh parsley
- ½ tsp. of salt
- ½ tsp. of pepper
- ½ tsp. of dehydrated garlic

Method

- Heat the olive oil in a skillet, add the scallions, shrimps and bell pepper and cook until the shrimp turns pink.
- Meanwhile, stir the eggs, whites, milk, salt, pepper, garlic and parsley in a large bowl until well blended.
- Distribute the shrimp and peppers evenly in the skillet and pour over the egg mixture.
- Cook for 4 minutes or until organic eggs set, turn and cook the other side.

Paleo Fish and Chips

Preparation time	30 minutes
Ready time	1hour
Serves	4
Serving quantity/unit	366 G / 13 ounces
Calories	569 Cal
Total Fat	28 g
Cholesterol	67 mg
Sodium	593 mg
Total Carbohydrates	55 g
Dietary fibers	11 g
Sugars	17 g
Protein	29 g
Vitamin C	0.78
Vitamin A	8.84
Iron	0.23
Calcium	0.21

Ingredients

Fish:

- 9 ounces of thick wild halibut fillets
- 2 tbsp. of coconut oil, melted
- 1 cup of almond flour
- 1 tbsp. of oregano
- 1 tbsp. of parsley
- ½ tsp. of salt
- ½ tsp. of dehydrated garlic
- ½ tsp. of pepper
- 1 organic egg, beaten
- 1/3 cup of almond milk

Chips:

- 8 sweet potatoes, thinly sliced
- 1 tbsp. of olive oil
- ¼ tsp. of salt

Method

- Fish:
- Transfer the flour to a mixing bowl and season with the salt, pepper, garlic, oregano and parsley. Stir to combine.
- Place the organic egg in a bowl and the milk on other.
- Heat the oil in a skillet.
- Dip each fish fillet into the milk and then toss them in the flour. Once this is done, carefully dip the fish fillets into the egg and then toss them one more time in the flour mixture.
- Fry the fillets in the coconut oil.

Chips:

- Preheat oven to 250F and line baking sheets with non-stick baking paper.
- Put the sweet potato slices, olive oil, and salt in a large bowl and toss to combine.
- Lay the sweet potato pieces in the baking sheets and bake for 45 minutes or until crisp.

Dinners

Roasted lamb

Preparation time	40 minutes
Ready time	5 hours
Serves	4
Serving quantity/unit	410 G / 14 ounces
Calories	543 Cal
Total Fat	33 g
Cholesterol	113 mg
Sodium	750 mg
Total Carbohydrates	23 g
Dietary fibers	6g
Sugars	9 g
Protein	35g
Vitamin C	0.39
Vitamin A	3.1
Iron	0.26
Calcium	0.11

Ingredients

- 1 ½ pounds of grass-fed leg of lamb, shank portion
- ¼ cup of olive oil
- 4 tbsps. of rosemary
- 1 tsp. of salt
- 1 tsp. of red pepper
- ½ cup of red wine
- ¼ cup of lemon juice

- 5 garlic cloves, cut into two pieces
- 2 tbsps. of crumbled bay leafs
- 6 carrots, sliced
- 3 onions, sliced

Method

- Place the meat on a large bowl and make small incisions around the leg with a sharp kitchen knife.
- Insert a garlic piece into each incision. Set aside.
- In a small bowl, combine the wine, lemon juice, rosemary and bay.
- Marinate the meat on the wine mixture for at least 3 hours in the refrigerator.
- Remove the meat from the refrigerator around 45 minutes before cooking.
- Preheat oven to 375F.
- Brush an oven-safe dish with half tablespoon of olive oil and arrange the onion and carrot slices evenly on the bottom of the dish.
- Spread the remaining olive oil around the meat.
- Transfer the meat and juices to the prepared oven-safe dish, and sprinkle with salt.
- Cover with aluminum foil and roast for 25-30 minutes.
- Remove the foil, lower the heat to 250F, and cook for one hour, or until meat is fully cooked, basting occasionally with the juices.
- Let the lamb leg rest for at least 15 minutes before slicing and serving.

Oven-baked salmon with cauliflower rice

Preparation time	5 minutes
Ready time	5 minutes
Serves	4
Serving quantity/unit	430 G / 15 ounces
Calories	493 Cal
Total Fat	30 g
Cholesterol	112 mg
Sodium	935 mg
Total Carbohydrates	13 g
Dietary fibers	6 g
Sugars	6 g
Protein	44 g
Vitamin C	1.94
Vitamin A	0.09
Iron	0.1
Calcium	0.08

Ingredients

Salmon:

- 4 wild Salmon fillets (150 to 180g each)
- 2 tbsps. of olive oil
- 4 tbsps. of parsley
- ½ tsp. of salt
- ¼ cup of lemon juice
- 2 tbsps. of classic Dijon mustard, unsweetened
- 1 garlic clove

Cauliflower rice:

- 1 large cauliflower head
- ½ tsp. of salt
- ½ tsp. of pepper
- ½ tsp. of dehydrated garlic, crushed

Method

- Salmon:
- Preheat oven to 375F.
- Cut 4 pieces of aluminum foil big enough to wrap the salmon covering it completely.
- In a small bowl combine the remaining ingredients to prepare the dressing.
- Place each salmon fillet on top of an aluminum sheet and distribute the dressing evenly on top of each fillet.
- Close the aluminum sheets and place the wraps on a baking sheet.
- Bake for 25 minutes. Remove from the oven and carefully check if the salmon is fully cooked. If necessary, cook for further 10-15 minutes.

Cauliflower rice:

- Place the cauliflower in a food processor and pulse until it is the size of rice.
- Transfer to a microwave-safe dish, season with salt and pepper, cover and microwave on high in periods of 5 minutes, until tender, stirring and verifying the cauliflower consistency between each cooking period.

Oven fried chicken drumsticks with sweet potatoes

Preparation time	5 minutes
Ready time	5 minutes
Serves	4
Serving quantity/unit	300 G / 11 ounces
Calories	495 Cal
Total Fat	21 g
Cholesterol	122 mg
Sodium	685 mg
Total Carbohydrates	46 g
Dietary fibers	8 g
Sugars	2 g
Protein	32 g
Vitamin C	0.46
Vitamin A	0.12
Iron	0.2
Calcium	0.09

Ingredients

- Drumsticks:
- 8 grass-fed chicken drumsticks
- ½ cup of almond flour
- 1 tbsp. of oregano
- 1 tbsp. of dried parsley
- ½ tsp. of pepper
- ¼ tsp. of garlic powder
- ½ tsp. of paprika
- ½ tsp. of salt
- 1 organic egg , beaten
- ¼ cup of almond milk

Sweet potato chips:

- 2 tbsp. of olive oil
- 4 cup of sweet potatoes, finely sliced
- 1/2 tsp. of salt
- 1/2 tsp. of pepper

Method

- Drumsticks:
- Preheat oven to 350F and line baking sheets with parchment paper.
- Transfer the flour to a mixing bowl and season with the salt, pepper, garlic, oregano paprika and parsley. Stir to combine.
- Place the egg in a bowl and the milk on other.
- Dip drumsticks into the milk and then toss them in the flour. Once this is done, carefully dip the drumsticks into the egg and then cover them one more time with the flour mixture.
- Lay the drumsticks in the baking sheets and bake for 30 minutes.
- Turn and bake for further 15 minutes or until the meat is fully cooked.

Sweet potato chips:

- Preheat oven to 250F and line baking sheets with non-stick baking paper.
- Put the sweet potato, olive oil, salt and pepper in a large bowl and toss to combine.
- Lay the sweet potato pieces in the baking sheets and bake for 45 minutes or until crisp.

Halibut fillet with parsnip puree

Preparation time	20 minutes
Ready time	50 minutes
Serves	1
Serving quantity/unit	530 G / 19 ounces
Calories	414 Cal
Total Fat	1.5 g
Cholesterol	47 mg
Sodium	159 mg
Total Carbohydrates	71.0 g
Dietary fibers	5.4g
Sugars	47.5 g
Protein	27.7g
Vitamin C	0.23
Vitamin A	0.01
Iron	0.01
Calcium	0.47

Ingredients

Halibut:

- 1 pound wild Halibut fillets
- 3 tbsps. of olive oil
- 3 garlic cloves, finely sliced
- 1 red jalapeno pepper, seeded and sliced
- ¼ cup of white wine
- 3 tbsps. of lemon juice
- 2 tbsps. of capers

Parsnip puree:

- 6 cups of parsnip
- 2 cups of cauliflower
- 4 garlic cloves
- 1 ½ tbsps. of clarified butter

Method

Halibut:

- Season the halibut with salt.
- Heat the oil in a skillet and cook the fish filets for 5-7 minutes on each side until lightly browned on both sides and fully cooked.
- Remove the fish from the skillet leaving the cooking juices.
- Add the garlic and jalapeno to the skillet where the fish was cooked and cook for half a minute.
- Add the wine and lemon juice. Bring to a boil and cook for further 2 minutes.
- Add the capers, stir and cook for another half a minute.
- Pour this sauce over the halibut fillets and serve immediately.

Parsnip puree:

- Wash, peel and slice the parsnips.
- Transfer the parsnips and cauliflower to a pot, cover with water, and season with salt.
- Bring water to a boil and cook for 15-20 minutes or until tender.
- Let cool, transfer the vegetables to a food processor and reserve some of the cooking liquid.
- Add the garlic and butter to the food processor and pulse until very smooth. Add a couple tablespoons of the cooking liquid to adjust the puree consistency if necessary.

Paleo Beef pie

Preparation time	20 minutes
Ready time	1h20m
Serves	4
Serving quantity/unit	410 G / 14 ounces
Calories	477 Cal
Total Fat	22 g
Cholesterol	116 mg
Sodium	436 mg
Total Carbohydrates	34 g
Dietary fibers	10g
Sugars	9 g
Protein	37g
Vitamin C	1
Vitamin A	0.19
Iron	0.3
Calcium	0.12

Ingredients

Beef layer:

- 1 pound of grass-fed ground beef, (95% lean meat / 5% fat)
- 1 cup of peeled tomatoes
- 1/2 tsp. of basil, finely chopped
- 1/2 tsp. of oregano
- 1/2 tsp. of paprika
- 1/2 tsp. of pepper
- 3 garlic cloves, finely chopped
- 1 onion, finely chopped
- 2 tbsp. of olive oil

Puree layer:

- 2 cups of cauliflower, chopped
- 4 cups of parsnips, chopped
- 1/2 tsp. of salt
- 3 garlic cloves,
- 2 tbsp. of clarified butter

Method

Beef layer:

- Heat the oil in a large skillet. Add the onion and garlic and cook until the onion is translucent.
- Add the beef and salt and cook, stirring, for 5 minutes until the meat starts to brown.
- Add the tomatoes and remaining seasons. Bring to a simmer and cook for 15-20 minutes until the volume of the pot content reduces slightly and it thickens a little.

Puree layer:

- Place the cauliflower and parsnip in a large pot and cover with water.
- Season with salt, bring to a boil and cook for 15-20 minutes, until the vegetables are tender.
- Remove from heat and let cool. Drain and reserve some of the cooking water.
- Combine the parsnips, cauliflower, garlic and clarified butter in a food processor and pulse until a smooth puree forms. If necessary adjust the consistency with a couple spoons of the cooking liquid.

Pie:

- Preheat oven to 375 degrees.
- Arrange the pie spreading the beef mixture evenly in the bottom of and oven safe dish and topping with the puree.
- Bake for 30 minutes or until the puree is golden.

Pork chops with apple chutney

Preparation time	15 minutes
Ready time	45 minutes
Serves	4
Serving quantity/unit	350 G / 12 ounces
Calories	490 Cal
Total Fat	16 g
Cholesterol	96 mg
Sodium	684 mg
Total Carbohydrates	56 g
Dietary fibers	5g
Sugars	45 g
Protein	34g
Vitamin C	0.17
Vitamin A	0.02
Iron	0.12
Calcium	0.05

Ingredients

Pork chops:

- 1 pound of grass-fed pork, chops (bone-in)
- ½ tsp. of salt
- ½ tsp. of black pepper
- 1 tsp. of crumbled bay leaf
- 3 garlic cloves

Apple chutney:

- 1 tbsp. of olive oil
- 6 cups of apple, cubed
- 2/3 cup of raisins
- ¼ cup of apple cider vinegar
- 3 tbsps. of raw honey
- 1 tbsp. of fresh ginger root, finely sliced
- ½ tsp. of salt
- 1 tsp. of classic Dijon mustard, unsweetened

Method

Pork chops:

- Preheat grill.
- Season the chops and grill them for 5 minutes on each side or until the meat is fully cooked.

Apple chutney:

- Heat the oil in a large skillet, add the apple and cook for 5 minutes or until it is light brown.
- Add the raisins and the remaining ingredients and cook over low heat for 10 minutes or until apples are fully cooked. Remove from heat.
- Serve the pork chops, while still warm, with the apple chutney on top.

Roasted sardines with baked sweet potato

Preparation time	25 minutes
Ready time	1h30 minutes
Serves	4
Serving quantity/unit	440 G / 16 ounces
Calories	620 Cal
Total Fat	31 g
Cholesterol	0 mg
Sodium	676 mg
Total Carbohydrates	55 g
Dietary fibers	9g
Sugars	17 g
Protein	29g
Vitamin C	1.04
Vitamin A	9.67
Iron	0.12
Calcium	0.11

Ingredients

Sardines:

- 1 pound of wild sardines
- ½ cup of white wine
- 1/3 cup of olive oil
- ½ tsp. of salt
- 5 garlic cloves
- ¼ cup of parsley
- ¼ cup of lemon juice
- 1 jalapeno pepper
- Sweet potato:
- 5 cups of sweet potatoes, peeled and cubed
- 1 tbsp. of olive oil
- ½ tsp. of salt

Method

- Sardines:
- Preheat oven to 375F.
- Combine the olive oil, garlic, parsley, lemon juice, salt and pepper in a mixing bowl.
- Pace the sardines in the bottom of an oven-safe dish big enough to arrange them in one single layer.
- Pour over the olive oil mixture, spreading it evenly through the sardines.
- Roast for 30-45 minutes or until fully cooked.
- Sweet potato:
- Preheat oven to 250F and line baking sheets with non-stick baking paper.
- Put the sweet potato, olive oil, salt and pepper in a large bowl and toss to combine.
- Lay the sweet potato pieces in the baking sheet and bake for 45 minutes or until crisp.

Desserts

Easy coconut and strawberry ice cream

Preparation time	5 minutes
Ready time	12 hours
Serves	1
Serving quantity/unit	117 G / 4 ounces
Calories	172 Cal
Total Fat	16 g
Cholesterol	0 mg
Sodium	3 mg
Total Carbohydrates	9 g
Dietary fibers	2g
Sugars	2 g
Protein	2g
Vitamin C	0.73
Vitamin A	0
Iron	0.07
Calcium	0.02

Ingredients

- ¾ cup of Coconut Cream
- 2 cups of strawberries

Method

- Combine the coconut cream and strawberries in a food processor until the strawberries are finely chopped and the mixture is smooth.
- Transfer into a bowl and freeze for 12 hours. (Stirring the ice cream occasionally during the freezing process will help to achieve a lighter and fluffier consistency).

Mango cookies

Preparation time	10 minutes
Ready time	25 minutes
Serves	4
Serving quantity/unit	50 G / 2 ounces
Calories	165 Cal
Total Fat	10 g
Cholesterol	0 mg
Sodium	26 mg
Total Carbohydrates	16 g
Dietary fibers	2g
Sugars	12 g
Protein	5g
Vitamin C	0
Vitamin A	0.03
Iron	0.04
Calcium	0.05

Ingredients

- 2/3 cup of almond flour
- 2 organic egg whites
- 1 tbsp. of coconut oil, melted
- 2 tbsps. of raw honey
- 3 dried mango slices, cut into small pieces

Method

- Preheat the oven to 350F.
- Line a baking sheet with non-stick baking paper.
- In a food processor combine the flour, egg whites, coconut oil and honey until smooth.
- Transfer to a mixing bowl and fold in the mango pieces.
- Scoop tablespoons of dough onto the prepared baking sheets and flatten each dough portion a little with your hands.
- Cook for 8-10 minutes or until golden.
- Remove from heat and let cool.

Apple pie

Preparation time	20 minutes
Ready time	1h15m
Serves	8
Serving quantity/unit	140 G / 5 ounces
Calories	174 Cal
Total Fat	8 g
Cholesterol	11 mg
Sodium	2 mg
Total Carbohydrates	27 g
Dietary fibers	4g
Sugars	21 g
Protein	2g
Vitamin C	0.09
Vitamin A	0.04
Iron	0.03
Calcium	0.04

Ingredients

- 5 apples, cored and thinly sliced
- 2 ½ + 1 ½ tbsps. of raw honey
- 2 tbsps. of water
- 2 tbsps. of cinnamon
- ½ cup of almond meal
- 3 tbsps. of clarified butter, melted

Method

- Preheat the oven to 370F.
- Combine two and a half tablespoons of honey with the water and cinnamon in a small bowl.
- Arrange one layer of apple slices in the bottom of a pie dish and brush it with the honey glaze.
- Repeat the process until all the apple slices are used. If any liquid remains, pour it over the top apple layer.
- In a food processor combine the almond meal, butter and the remaining honey just until well blended.
- Spread the almond meal mixture on top of the apple layers and bake for 45-50 minutes, or until the apples are tender and the almond meal crust is golden.

Minty Watermelon Sorbet

Preparation time	10 minutes
Ready time	4 hours
Serves	4
Serving quantity/unit	261 G / 9 ounces
Calories	90 Cal
Total Fat	0 g
Cholesterol	0 mg
Sodium	5 mg
Total Carbohydrates	23 g
Dietary fibers	1g
Sugars	20 g
Protein	1g
Vitamin C	0.26
Vitamin A	0.23
Iron	0.04
Calcium	0.02

Ingredients

- 5 cups of seedless watermelon, cubed
- 2 tbsps. of raw honey
- 1 cup of ice
- 1 tbsp. of mint

Method

- Combine all the ingredients in a food processor.
- Transfer to a metal container, cover and freeze for 3-4 hours or until it is hard on the outside and slushy in the center.

Carrot and pecans cake

Preparation time	15 minutes
Ready time	1 hour
Serves	10
Serving quantity/unit	85 G / 3 ounces
Calories	222 Cal
Total Fat	17 g
Cholesterol	65 mg
Sodium	180 mg
Total Carbohydrates	13 g
Dietary fibers	3g
Sugars	9 g
Protein	7g
Vitamin C	0.01
Vitamin A	0.55
Iron	0.07
Calcium	0.06

Ingredients

- 1 ½ cups of almond flour
- 4 organic eggs, yolks and whites separated
- 2 organic egg whites
- 4 tbsp. of raw honey
- 1 cup of carrots, boiled
- 1 tbsp. of cinnamon
- ¼ cup of pecan,
- ¼ cup of olive oil
- ½ cup of almond milk
- 1 tsp. of baking soda

Method

- Preheat the oven to 350°F.
- Process the pecan nuts in a food processor until they are coarsely chopped.
- Combine the yolks, 3 tablespoons of oil and honey in a large bowl and add the milk.
- Mash the carrot and add it to the egg mixture, stir until well blended. Add the nuts.
- Mix flour with baking soda, and cinnamon and add to the egg mixture.
- Beat the egg whites until stiff and carefully fold them in the cake batter.
- Grease a cake pan with the remaining oil and line it with non-stick baking paper.
- Pour in the batter and bake for 45 minutes or until a toothpick comes out clean.

Warm coconut and chocolate pudding

Preparation time	5 minutes
Ready time	35 minutes
Serves	4
Serving quantity/unit	100 G / 4 ounces
Calories	210 Cal
Total Fat	16 g
Cholesterol	43 mg
Sodium	37 mg
Total Carbohydrates	19 g
Dietary fibers	5g
Sugars	12 g
Protein	6g
Vitamin C	0.02
Vitamin A	0.02
Iron	0.16
Calcium	0.07

Ingredients

- ¾ cup of coconut milk
- ½ cup of raw cocoa
- 2 tbsps. of raw honey
- 1 organic egg, beaten
- 2 tbsps. of almond flour
- ½ cup of grass-fed milk or almond milk

Method

- Combine all the ingredients in a large pan.
- Bring it to a simmer over low heat and cook for 5-7 minutes, or more if you prefer a thicker consistency, whisking continuously. Don't let it boil.
- Remove saucepan from heat. Let cool for 15 minutes and transfer the mixture into serving plates.

Cocoa meringues with coconut cream and blueberries

Preparation time	5 minutes
Ready time	5 minutes
Serves	4
Serving quantity/unit	80 G / 3 ounces
Calories	117 Cal
Total Fat	6 g
Cholesterol	0 mg
Sodium	57 mg
Total Carbohydrates	15 g
Dietary fibers	2 g
Sugars	11 g
Protein	5 g
Vitamin C	0.04
Vitamin A	0
Iron	0.06
Calcium	0.01

Ingredients

Meringues:

- 4 organic egg whites
- 3 tbsp. of raw cocoa
- Blueberry syrup:
- 2 tbsp. of raw honey
- 1/2 cup of blueberries
- 1 tbsp. of water

Serve with:

- 4 tbsp. of coconut cream

Method

Meringues:

- Preheat oven to 275F.
- Beat the egg whites until stiff and carefully fold in the cocoa.
- Scoop the mixture onto baking sheets lined with non-stick parchment paper and cook for 30-40 minutes.

Blueberry syrup:

- Combine the blueberries and water in a medium saucepan and bring to a simmer.
- Simmer for 10-15 minutes or until the blueberries are soft and the syrup thickens, add the raw honey, stir, and remove from heat.
- Serve the meringues topped with the blueberry sauce and coconut cream.

Exclusive Bonus Download: Crossfit to Drop Fat

Download your bonus, please visit the download link above from your PC or MAC. To open PDF files, visit http://get.adobe.com/reader/ to download the reader if it's not already installed on your PC or Mac. To open ZIP files, you may need to download WinZip from http://www.winzip.com. This download is for PC or Mac ONLY and might not be downloadable to kindle.

CrossFit is the principal strength and conditioning program for many police academies and tactical operations teams, military special operations units, champion martial artists, and hundreds of other elite and professional athletes worldwide.

Inside this ebook you will learn:

- The history of Cross fit training
- What is Cross fit training
- Advice on how to live life to the fullest yet still shred pounds
- Practical advice on the best exercises for cross fit
- The benefits of cross fit training
- Tips to help you succeed
- and more...

Visit the URL above to download this guide and start achieving your weight loss and fitness goals NOW

One Last Thing...

Thank you so much for reading my book. I hope you really liked it. As you probably know, many people look at the reviews on Amazon before they decide to purchase a book. If you liked the book, could you please take a minute to leave a review with your feedback? 60 seconds is all I'm asking for, and it would mean the world to me.

Books by Lars Andersen

The Smoothies for Runners Book

Juices for Runners

Smoothies for Cyclists

Juices for Cyclists

Paleo Diet for Cyclists

Smoothies for Triathletes

Juices for Triathletes

Paleo Diet for Triathletes

Smoothies for Strength

About the Author

Lars Andersen is a sports author, nutritional researcher and fitness enthusiast. In his spare time he participates in competitive running, swimming and cycling events and enjoys hiking with his two border collies.

Lars Andersen

Published by Nordic Standard Publishing

Atlanta, Georgia USA

NORDICSTANDARD
PUBLISHING

4699710R00042

Printed in Great Britain
by Amazon.co.uk, Ltd.,
Marston Gate.